ASOGWA JOY LOVE

Tides of Understanding

Copyright © 2024 by Asogwa Joy Love

All rights reserved. No part of this publication may be reproduced, stored or transmitted in any form or by any means, electronic, mechanical, photocopying, recording, scanning, or otherwise without written permission from the publisher. It is illegal to copy this book, post it to a website, or distribute it by any other means without permission.

Asogwa Joy Love asserts the moral right to be identified as the author of this work.

Asogwa Joy Love has no responsibility for the persistence or accuracy of URLs for external or third-party Internet Websites referred to in this publication and does not guarantee that any content on such Websites is, or will remain, accurate or appropriate.

First edition

This book was professionally typeset on Reedsy.
Find out more at reedsy.com

Contents

1	Echoes of the Past	1
2	The Unseen Rift	5
3	Shadows of Deceit	9
4	The Missing Link	13
5	Crossed Paths	18
6	The Hidden Archive	23
7	Fractured Trust	28
8	The Unseen Hand	33
9	The Unseen Hand	38
10	Echoes of the Past	43
11	The Veil Lifts	48
12	The Architect's Labyrinth	53

1

Echoes of the Past

The rain pattered relentlessly against the windowpanes of the old Victorian house, casting a muted glow across the room. Inside, Ella sat by the fireplace, her fingers tracing the edges of a weathered photo album. The soft crackle of the logs was the only sound accompanying her as she flipped through the pages, each snapshot a silent witness to moments long gone. Her heart ached with nostalgia and a sense of foreboding that she couldn't shake.

Her husband, Tom, entered the room, shaking off the last remnants of the storm from his coat. He glanced over at her with a faint smile, though his eyes were clouded with exhaustion from a long day at the office. "Still at it?" he asked, trying to sound lighthearted but failing to mask the weariness in his voice.

Ella nodded, her gaze fixed on a photograph of her parents, taken years before she had met Tom. "Just looking at some old pictures. It's been a while since I've done this."

Tom moved to stand beside her, peering down at the album. "Everything okay?"

Ella hesitated, her fingers pausing over a particularly old photo of her mother in a vibrant red dress. There was something about that picture—a sense of joy and freedom that seemed distant now. "Yeah, just reminiscing."

Tom's eyes lingered on her face, sensing an undercurrent of unease. He placed a hand on her shoulder, offering a reassuring squeeze. "You know you can talk to me about anything, right?"

Ella managed a faint smile, though it didn't reach her eyes. "I know. It's just... there's something unsettling about these memories. Like they're trying to tell me something I don't understand."

Before Tom could respond, the doorbell rang sharply, slicing through the calm of the evening. Ella's face paled as she looked toward the door. "Who could that be at this hour?"

Tom frowned, glancing at his watch. "I'll get it."

He walked to the door, opening it to reveal a figure shrouded in the dark of the stormy night. The person's face was obscured by the brim of a wide-brimmed hat, but the glint of recognition flashed in Tom's eyes. He stepped aside, allowing the visitor inside.

Ella's curiosity grew as she watched Tom exchange a few words with the stranger, whose voice was low and gravelly. The visitor finally removed the hat, revealing a face she hadn't seen in years—Mark, her estranged brother. His appearance was a shock, his once-familiar features now hardened and worn by time.

"Mark?" Ella's voice wavered as she took in his appearance. "What are you doing here?"

Mark looked around the room, his eyes settling on the photo album on the table. "Ella, we need to talk."

Tom glanced between them, sensing the tension that crackled in the air. "I'll leave you two to catch up," he said, though his concern was evident. He offered a reassuring pat on Ella's shoulder before retreating to the kitchen.

Ella motioned for Mark to sit, though her hands trembled slightly as she moved to fetch him a drink. "This is a surprise. The last time we spoke, things weren't..."

"Good between us," Mark finished for her, sitting down heavily in an armchair. "I know. And I'm sorry for that."

Ella studied his face, noting the deep lines and the shadows under his eyes. "You look like you've been through a lot. What's going on?"

Mark's gaze was steady, but there was a haunted look in his eyes. "I didn't come here just to catch up. There's something you need to know, something I should have told you a long time ago."

Ella's heart quickened. "What is it?"

Mark took a deep breath, his fingers gripping the armrests of the chair. "It's about Mom and Dad. There was something they were involved in... something dangerous."

Ella's breath caught in her throat. "Dangerous? What do you mean?"

Mark's eyes were intense as he continued, "I didn't understand it all at the time, but I've been piecing things together. They were involved in something that put them in a lot of danger, and I think... I think it might have led to their deaths."

Ella recoiled slightly, her mind racing with questions. "Why didn't you tell me this before? Why now?"

"I thought I could protect you by keeping you in the dark," Mark said, his voice heavy with regret. "But I've learned that keeping secrets only makes things worse. I've been getting threats—messages warning me to stay away from this. They know I'm looking into it, and now…"

A chill ran down Ella's spine. "And now?"

Mark's face grew grim. "Now I'm afraid they might come after you too."

The room seemed to close in around Ella as she absorbed the weight of Mark's words. The familiar sense of nostalgia from the photo album now felt like a cruel reminder of a past that was far from peaceful. The storm outside intensified, and Ella's mind raced with the implications of what Mark had revealed. The safe, comforting world she had built with Tom was suddenly threatened by shadows from the past.

Mark's presence was a stark reminder that the past wasn't as distant as she'd hoped. As the rain lashed against the windows, Ella knew that the calm facade of her life was about to be shattered, and the tides of understanding were about to pull her into a turbulent sea of secrets and danger.

2

The Unseen Rift

Ella lay in bed, her mind unable to settle from the revelations of the previous night. The shadows of the room seemed to deepen with every tick of the clock, each second amplifying the anxiety that gripped her. Tom, fast asleep beside her, had turned off the bedside lamp before drifting off, but Ella's eyes remained wide open, staring into the darkness.

The rain had stopped, leaving an eerie silence that felt almost too still. Ella's thoughts swirled around Mark's visit and the implications of his warnings. The photo album lay on the bedside table, its pages open to the picture of her parents. She reached over and closed it, trying to push away the unsettling thoughts. Yet, the more she tried to focus on the quiet comfort of her room, the more her thoughts twisted into a spiral of dread.

Tom's steady breathing beside her was a contrast to the storm raging in her mind. She turned to look at him, his face serene in sleep, and she wondered how he would react to the truth about her past. The burden of Mark's words felt too heavy to share, and the fear of what might come next was almost paralyzing.

At that moment, a faint, unfamiliar noise interrupted the silence. It was a soft, persistent scratching sound, coming from downstairs. Ella's heart raced, her instincts screaming that something was wrong. She carefully eased out of bed, trying not to wake Tom. Wrapped in a robe, she tiptoed to the bedroom door and paused, listening intently.

The sound was still there, more pronounced now—a rhythmic scratching that seemed to come from the direction of the living room. Ella's breath caught in her throat as she inched toward the staircase, each step amplified in the quiet house. She made her way down the stairs, clutching the railing for support, her mind racing with possibilities.

The house was dark, save for the faint moonlight filtering through the windows. The scratching noise grew louder as she approached the living room. Ella reached for the light switch but hesitated, her hand trembling. Instead, she crept closer, peeking through the crack of the slightly ajar door.

The room was dimly lit by the moonlight, and at first glance, everything seemed in order. But as she scanned the room, her eyes were drawn to the old grandfather clock in the corner. The scratching sound was definitely coming from behind it. Ella's pulse quickened as she approached the clock. She carefully moved it aside, revealing a small, dusty safe embedded into the wall—a safe that had been hidden behind the clock for as long as she could remember.

The safe wasn't something Ella had ever given much thought to; it had always been there, a relic of the past. She crouched down and examined it closely, noticing that it had been tampered with. The once-matching paint was scratched, and the lock seemed slightly ajar. A wave of realization hit her: someone had been trying to open it.

Just as she was about to investigate further, a sudden noise from the hallway made her freeze. Her heart pounded in her chest as she listened intently. The sound was unmistakable—footsteps. Heavy and deliberate, moving toward the living room. Ella quickly pushed the clock back into place and took a step back, her mind racing. She needed to hide.

She darted behind the curtains, holding her breath as the footsteps grew closer. Her heart felt as though it might burst from her chest. The door to the living room creaked open slowly, and a shadow fell across the floor. Ella squinted through the gap in the curtains, trying to make out the figure that had entered.

The intruder was cloaked in darkness, but Ella could make out the silhouette of a man. He moved with purpose, heading straight for the clock. Ella's hand went to her mouth to stifle a gasp as he began to inspect the area where she had just been. The man's movements were methodical, almost as if he were looking for something specific.

Ella's mind raced. Was this person connected to the threats Mark had mentioned? Was this an enemy from her past, or something more sinister? Her fear intensified as the man's flashlight beam danced over the area she had disturbed. She could see his face now, illuminated briefly by the flashlight—a face that was unfamiliar yet menacing.

Her mind spun with thoughts of what to do next. She considered making a run for it, but the thought of alerting the intruder to her presence was terrifying. She needed to find a way to protect herself and Tom, and she needed answers. Ella slowly and carefully pulled out her phone, trying not to make any noise as she dialed Tom's number.

Her fingers shook as she pressed the call button, holding her breath as the phone rang softly. The intruder was too focused on the safe to notice her movement. The call went straight to voicemail, and Ella's heart sank. She had to think fast.

As the intruder continued to search the room, Ella quietly stepped back and made her way toward the kitchen. Her footsteps were light, and she hoped that the intruder would remain engrossed in his search. Reaching the kitchen, she grabbed a heavy flashlight from the counter and took a deep breath, preparing herself to confront whatever danger lay ahead.

With the flashlight in hand, Ella turned back toward the living room. The intruder was still at the safe, clearly frustrated by his lack of progress. Ella knew she had to act quickly. She carefully positioned herself behind a nearby wall, waiting for the right moment to shine the flashlight and confront the intruder.

As she prepared to make her move, a sudden noise upstairs made her freeze. Tom was awake. The sound of him moving around in the bedroom was unmistakable, and Ella's heart sank as she realized he might be in danger too.

She had to warn him and protect her home, but with the intruder so close, every decision carried a risk. Ella took a deep breath, steeling herself for the confrontation ahead, and prepared to face the unknown dangers that had suddenly intruded upon their lives.

3

Shadows of Deceit

Ella's hands trembled as she clutched the heavy flashlight, her breath coming in shallow, quick bursts. The sound of Tom moving upstairs had intensified her sense of urgency, but she couldn't risk drawing attention to herself prematurely. The intruder was still occupied with the safe, his flashlight casting erratic beams across the room as he struggled with the lock.

She took a deep breath and crept back into the living room, her mind racing through every possible scenario. The man's back was turned, giving her a fleeting opportunity to act. Ella moved silently, positioning herself behind a large armchair that was obscured by shadows. She tightened her grip on the flashlight, ready to use it if necessary.

Tom's footsteps grew louder upstairs, and Ella's anxiety spiked. She needed to make a decision quickly. If the intruder heard Tom, he might act unpredictably. As she steeled herself, the man's voice suddenly broke the silence.

"I know you're here, Ella."

The cold, chilling tone made Ella's blood run cold. Her heart pounded in her chest, and she stifled a gasp. How could he possibly know her name? The intruder had clearly done his homework, and the realization that she was dealing with someone who knew far too much about her sent a shiver down her spine.

"I don't want to hurt anyone," the intruder continued, his voice muffled but unmistakably threatening. "Just give me what I'm looking for, and we can avoid any more trouble."

Ella's mind raced as she tried to piece together the intruder's intentions. What could he be searching for in the safe that was so important? And why was he targeting her?

Desperate to protect Tom and herself, Ella decided to act. She moved silently from behind the armchair and approached the intruder from the side. Her heart thudded in her ears as she raised the flashlight, preparing to strike if necessary.

Just as she was about to swing, the intruder's phone buzzed, and he answered it with an irritated grunt. "What?" he snapped into the phone, his voice barely audible. "I'm in the middle of something. This better be important."

Ella used the distraction to her advantage, slipping behind the intruder and positioning herself closer to the safe. The man's conversation was a one-sided affair, filled with impatient responses and terse commands.

A sudden clatter from upstairs made Ella freeze. She heard Tom's voice, raised in confusion. Panic surged through her. Tom must have heard the intruder or the commotion in the living room. She had to get to him before it was too late.

Ella carefully retreated to the hallway, making sure to keep her movements as quiet as possible. Her heart raced as she climbed the stairs, her flashlight illuminating the path ahead. Each step felt like a mile, and her anxiety mounted with every creak of the old wooden steps.

As she reached the top of the stairs, she saw Tom standing in the bedroom doorway, looking bewildered. "Ella?" he called out softly, his voice tinged with concern. "What's going on?"

Ella rushed to him, grabbing his arm. "Tom, there's someone downstairs. We need to get out of here, now."

Tom's eyes widened in alarm. "What? How did you—"

"Later," Ella interrupted urgently. "There's no time. We need to get out before he realizes we're up here."

Tom looked around, his expression a mix of confusion and fear. "What about the safe? What's he after?"

"We can't worry about that right now," Ella said, pulling him toward the window. "We have to find a way to get out of the house."

They moved quickly, Tom still in his pajamas, as they climbed out of the bedroom window onto the sloped roof below. Ella's heart raced as they carefully made their way to the edge of the roof, the moonlight casting eerie shadows over the yard.

From their vantage point, they could see the intruder moving around the living room, clearly frustrated. Ella's flashlight was still in her hand, and she hoped it hadn't been noticed. As they reached the edge of the roof, Tom's face was pale with fear.

"How do we get down?" he asked, his voice barely a whisper.

Ella scanned the area and spotted a sturdy tree close to the ground. "We can use the tree to climb down. Just be careful."

They carefully descended the tree, branch by branch, their movements slow and deliberate. The intruder's voice drifted up from the house, and Ella's nerves were on edge. She glanced back toward the window, seeing the man's silhouette illuminated by the living room light. He was still searching, oblivious to their escape.

Once they were safely on the ground, Ella led Tom to the side of the house, away from the intruder's line of sight. They crouched behind a row of bushes, catching their breath.

"What's going on?" Tom asked, his voice trembling. "Who was that man, and what does he want?"

Ella took a deep breath, trying to steady her racing thoughts. "It's connected to my past, to what Mark warned me about. I don't have all the answers yet, but we need to figure out what's going on and how to stay safe."

Tom nodded, his face set in determination. "We'll get through this. But we need a plan."

Ella glanced back at the house, her mind racing. The intruder's presence was a terrifying reminder of the dangers lurking in the shadows of her past. The unknown threat had shattered their sense of security, and the only way forward was to confront the darkness head-on. She took Tom's hand, squeezing it tightly. They were in this together, and they needed to stay one step ahead of the danger that had intruded upon their lives.

4

The Missing Link

The early morning light filtered through the dense canopy of trees surrounding the Victorian house, casting dappled shadows across the garden. Ella and Tom had spent the night huddled in the bushes, adrenaline still coursing through their veins. With dawn breaking, they knew they needed to move quickly, but the fear of returning to the house was overwhelming. The intruder might still be inside, or worse, he might have left a trap.

Tom stood up, brushing dirt off his pajamas. "We need to get to the police," he said, his voice strained but determined. "They can help us figure out who this guy is and what he wants."

Ella nodded, her mind still racing. "Yes, but we need to be careful. If the intruder is connected to my past, he might have ties to people who know where we are."

They made their way to Tom's car, parked on the street outside the property, careful to avoid any paths that might be watched. The car was an old model with a few dings and scratches, a stark contrast to the pristine condition of the house they had just fled. Ella glanced back at the Victorian house, its once-comforting facade now a symbol of the danger that lurked within.

As Tom started the car, Ella's phone buzzed in her pocket. She fished it out, her heart skipping a beat when she saw the notification: a message from Mark. Her fingers trembled as she opened it, the message brief but chilling: "They're after something specific. Find the missing link."

Ella's breath caught in her throat. What could Mark mean by "the missing link"? Her thoughts raced back to the safe behind the grandfather clock. What could be so important that someone would break into their home and search for it?

Tom noticed her distress. "What's wrong?"

"Mark sent me a message," Ella said, her voice shaky. "He said, 'Find the missing link.' I don't understand what he's referring to, but it might be related to the safe."

Tom's expression grew serious. "Then we need to get back in there and figure out what's inside that safe."

They arrived at the local police station, the sun now high in the sky. The station was a modest building, its front entrance bustling with activity as officers and civilians moved about. They were greeted by a receptionist who directed them to a waiting area. After a short wait, Detective Harris, a tall man with a stern face, approached them.

"Mr. and Mrs. Walker?" he asked, looking at them with a mixture of curiosity and concern.

"Yes," Ella replied. "We need to report a break-in. There was an intruder in our home last night."

Detective Harris led them to a private room where they recounted the events. Ella tried to provide as much detail as possible, describing the intruder and the strange message from Mark. Detective Harris listened intently, taking notes and asking clarifying questions.

"Do you have any idea what the intruder was looking for?" he asked, his tone serious.

Ella hesitated, glancing at Tom. "We think it might be related to something in our house—a safe behind a grandfather clock. It's been there for as long as I can remember, but I don't know what's inside."

Detective Harris nodded. "I'll send a team to your house to investigate. In the meantime, it's important that you remain vigilant. If you receive any more messages or see anything suspicious, contact us immediately."

Ella and Tom left the station, their minds still swirling with confusion and fear. They decided to return to the house, determined to find out what was inside the safe. As they approached the Victorian house, Ella's anxiety grew. Every creak of the porch and every gust of wind felt like a potential threat.

They entered cautiously, Tom leading the way. The house was eerily quiet, the only sound being the occasional drip of water from the leaky roof. Ella's eyes were drawn to the living room, where the grandfather clock still stood. The sight of it made her stomach churn.

Tom approached the clock, inspecting it closely. "We need to open the safe and see what's inside. It might give us some answers."

Ella nodded, her hands trembling as she watched Tom work on the safe. The lock had been damaged during the intruder's search, and Tom struggled to pry it open. With a final, frustrated grunt, he managed to force the safe open.

Inside, there were several items packed tightly: old documents, faded photographs, and a small, leather-bound journal. Ella's heart raced as she carefully removed the journal from the safe. Its cover was cracked and worn, but the clasp was intact. She opened it cautiously, revealing pages filled with neat handwriting.

Ella began to read aloud, her voice shaking. "This is a journal from my mother. It looks like it details various events and… wait, here's a reference to something called 'The Link.'"

Tom looked over her shoulder, his expression growing concerned. "What does it say?"

Ella scanned the pages, her eyes widening as she read the entry. "It mentions a 'link' that connects to something important—something that could put our family at risk. But there are no specifics, just vague references."

The journal's pages were filled with cryptic notes and references to "The Link," but nothing concrete. Ella felt a surge of frustration. The journal didn't seem to provide any clear answers, just more questions.

Tom paced the room, his anxiety palpable. "What now? If the journal isn't helping, where do we go from here?"

Ella thought for a moment, then glanced at the photographs in the safe. She picked up a photo of her parents and studied it closely. There was something familiar about the image, but she couldn't quite place it.

As she turned the photo over, she noticed something scrawled in faint ink on the back: an address.

"This might be a clue," Ella said, her voice filled with hope. "The address on this photo—it could lead us to something important."

Tom nodded, determination in his eyes. "Then we need to investigate. Let's find out where this address leads and what it has to do with all of this."

They gathered the documents and the journal, determined to follow the lead. As they left the house, Ella felt a mix of apprehension and resolve. The missing link was out there, and it was their only hope of unraveling the mystery that had suddenly engulfed their lives.

5

Crossed Paths

Ella and Tom navigated through the narrow streets of the city, the address on the back of the photograph clutched tightly in Ella's hand. The sun had dipped below the horizon, and the streetlights cast long shadows that seemed to stretch and twist like dark fingers reaching for them. The address led them to an old warehouse district, an area that had seen better days. The buildings were aged, their facades marred by graffiti and grime. The streets were eerily quiet, the silence punctuated only by the distant hum of traffic.

Tom drove cautiously, his eyes scanning the surroundings for any signs of activity. The warehouse they were looking for was at the end of a desolate alley, obscured by an overgrown hedge and a rusting gate. As they approached, Ella felt a knot tighten in her stomach. The place looked abandoned, but she knew better than to let appearances deceive her.

"This is it," Tom said, parking the car a safe distance away. He turned to Ella, his face set in a grim expression. "We should check it out, but we need to be careful. There's no telling what we might find."

Ella nodded, her heart pounding in her chest. They exited the car and approached the warehouse on foot. The area was dimly lit by a few scattered streetlamps, casting an unsettling glow over the scene. The warehouse itself loomed ahead, its broken windows and sagging roof giving it an almost menacing presence.

Ella led the way, her flashlight cutting through the darkness as they approached the entrance. The gate was ajar, hanging precariously on its hinges. Tom pushed it open, the metal scraping against the ground with a loud, grating noise that echoed through the alley. They winced at the sound, knowing it might attract unwanted attention.

Inside, the warehouse was a cavernous space, filled with old crates, discarded machinery, and dust-covered debris. The air was thick with the smell of rust and decay. Ella's flashlight beam danced across the walls, revealing faded murals and broken glass scattered on the floor.

"Stay close," Ella whispered, her voice barely audible. "We don't know what we're walking into."

Tom followed closely, his flashlight revealing a makeshift path through the clutter. They moved cautiously, every creak of the floorboards heightening their sense of vulnerability. Ella's thoughts raced, trying to piece together what might be hidden in this forsaken place and how it related to the mysterious journal and the intruder's pursuit.

They reached a large, open space in the center of the warehouse. It appeared to be the main area, with high ceilings and a large, rusted crane hanging overhead. The beams of their flashlights swept across the room, revealing a series of old filing cabinets and shelves. On one of the shelves, Ella spotted something that made her stop in her tracks—a familiar, ornate box that resembled the one her mother used to keep.

"Tom, look at that," Ella said, her voice tinged with excitement and apprehension. "That box... it looks like it might be important."

They approached the box with caution. Ella reached out to open it, her fingers trembling. The box was heavy and ornate, with intricate carvings that seemed to tell a story of their own. She carefully lifted the lid, revealing a stack of documents and a few personal items.

As Ella sifted through the contents, she found a series of old photographs, some of which were similar to the ones in the safe but with additional people and locations. One photograph stood out—a picture of her mother standing with a man she didn't recognize. The man was older, with a stern expression, and the background suggested they were in a different location altogether.

"Who's this?" Tom asked, peering over her shoulder.

"I don't know," Ella replied, her brow furrowed. "But he must be connected to whatever this is."

Ella continued to examine the documents, finding several handwritten notes that mentioned meetings, codes, and transactions. The notes were cryptic, but they hinted at a network of people and a covert operation that her mother might have been involved in. Her heart raced as she pieced together fragments of information, realizing that the past her mother was involved in was far more complex and dangerous than she had ever imagined.

Suddenly, a noise behind them made Ella and Tom freeze. The sound of footsteps echoed through the warehouse, growing louder and closer. Ella's pulse quickened as she turned off her flashlight and motioned for Tom to follow her. They ducked behind a stack of crates, their breaths coming in shallow gasps.

The footsteps grew nearer, and Ella strained to listen. The intruder from the previous night—or someone associated with him—was clearly in the warehouse. They could hear the sound of muffled voices and the rustling of objects being moved.

Tom glanced at Ella, his eyes wide with fear. "We need to get out of here. If they catch us, we're in serious trouble."

Ella nodded in agreement. They carefully made their way toward the back of the warehouse, trying to remain as silent as possible. The footsteps continued to draw closer, and Ella's heart raced with each passing second. They reached a side exit, slightly ajar, and Ella pushed it open, leading Tom out into the cool night air.

As they made their way back to the car, Ella's mind raced with the implications of what they had discovered. The warehouse had revealed pieces of a larger puzzle, but it also introduced a new layer of danger. The fact that someone else was searching for the same information only heightened their sense of urgency.

Once they were safely back in the car, Tom started the engine, and they drove away from the warehouse. Ella glanced in the rearview mirror, her heart still pounding, and hoped that they hadn't been followed.

"What now?" Tom asked, breaking the silence.

"We need to figure out who the man in the photograph is and why he was important," Ella replied, her voice steady but filled with determination. "We need to understand the full picture before we can figure out how to protect ourselves."

As they drove through the darkened streets, Ella felt a growing resolve. The pieces of the mystery were slowly coming together, but the danger was far from over. The shadows of deceit were closing in, and Ella knew that unraveling the truth would be their only way to find safety and understand the true extent of the threats they faced.

6

The Hidden Archive

Ella and Tom returned to their temporary apartment, the weight of their discoveries pressing heavily on their minds. The photograph of Ella's mother with the mysterious man and the documents from the warehouse were scattered across the dining table. Ella sat at the table, staring at the photograph with a mixture of frustration and determination. The warehouse had yielded some answers but left them with more questions than they had started with.

Tom paced the small living room, his anxiety evident in his movements. "We need to find out who that man is. It's clear he's connected to all this, but we don't have a clue about his identity or role."

Ella nodded, her gaze fixed on the photograph. "I agree. We also need to dig deeper into the documents. They might contain clues about where to find more information."

Tom stopped pacing and sat across from Ella. "Where do we start? We don't even know where to look."

Ella took a deep breath, her mind racing through the possibilities. "The documents mentioned a 'hidden archive' several times. Maybe it's a location or a database related to the network my mother was involved in."

Tom's eyes lit up with a mix of hope and skepticism. "A hidden archive? That sounds like something out of a spy novel."

"It might be," Ella said, her voice steady. "But given the circumstances, it could be our best lead."

They turned their attention to the documents, sifting through the handwritten notes and references. One of the notes contained a series of numbers and letters that seemed to form a code. Ella and Tom worked together to decode it, their eyes straining under the dim light of the apartment.

After several hours of painstaking effort, they managed to crack the code. It revealed an address and a set of instructions that seemed to be directions to a specific location. The address led them to an old, abandoned building on the outskirts of town—a place that seemed to fit the description of a hidden archive.

As dawn approached, Ella and Tom decided to investigate. They drove to the address, the early morning mist hanging over the landscape. The building was a nondescript warehouse, much like the one they had visited before, but it looked older and more decrepit. The windows were boarded up, and the door was secured with a heavy padlock.

Tom parked the car a safe distance away, and they approached the building cautiously. The air was chilly, and the only sounds were the distant chirping of birds and the rustling of leaves. Ella's nerves were on edge, knowing that they were about to uncover something that could be dangerous.

"We need to find a way in," Ella said, her voice low and tense. "But we should be careful. The intruder might have left behind traps or security measures."

Tom nodded, and they began searching the perimeter of the building. They found a side entrance that was partially open, its lock rusted and weak. With some effort, Tom managed to pry it open, revealing a dark, musty interior.

Inside, the warehouse was filled with old filing cabinets, dusty boxes, and shelves lined with forgotten items. The air was thick with the smell of mildew and decay. Ella and Tom moved cautiously, their flashlights cutting through the darkness as they explored the space.

The warehouse was enormous, with rows of shelves stretching as far as the eye could see. The silence was almost oppressive, and every sound seemed magnified in the empty space. Ella's flashlight beam fell on a sign hanging from the ceiling that read "Restricted Access." Her heart skipped a beat—this might be the archive they were looking for.

They continued deeper into the warehouse, navigating through the cluttered aisles. The documents they had decoded mentioned a specific section of the archive that was supposed to contain important information. Ella hoped that finding this section would bring them closer to understanding the mystery.

After what felt like hours of searching, they finally came upon a small, locked room tucked away at the back of the warehouse. The door was secured with a sophisticated locking mechanism, unlike the other, more basic locks they had encountered.

Tom examined the lock, his brow furrowed in concentration. "This looks like it might require a code or key. We might need to find the right combination to open it."

Ella glanced around, her eyes scanning the room for any clues. On one of the nearby shelves, she noticed a series of old, dusty ledgers. She carefully pulled one out and began flipping through the pages, hoping to find something useful.

As she examined the ledgers, Ella found a set of notes that seemed to match the format of the code they had cracked earlier. She copied down a few sequences that appeared to be related to the lock. Tom tried these sequences on the locking mechanism, and with a satisfying click, the door creaked open.

Inside, the room was filled with neatly organized files, documents, and several large boxes. Ella and Tom entered, their flashlights illuminating the contents. The room appeared to be a central repository for important documents and records.

Ella's eyes fell on a large, metal cabinet in the corner of the room. It was locked with a heavy padlock, and the keyhole looked old and intricate. She felt a surge of hope. If the cabinet contained crucial information, it could provide the answers they were seeking.

Tom approached the cabinet and tried to pick the lock, using a set of tools he had brought with him. After several tense minutes of careful manipulation, the padlock clicked open, and Tom lifted the lid.

Inside the cabinet, Ella found a collection of files and a few more boxes. One of the files was labeled with her mother's name, and her heart raced as she pulled it out. The file was filled with documents, photographs, and handwritten notes that seemed to detail her mother's involvement in the covert network.

As Ella began to read through the documents, she realized that they contained detailed accounts of various operations, including coded messages and references to key individuals. The information was dense and complex, but it was clear that her mother had been deeply involved in something significant.

The most startling discovery was a letter addressed to Ella. It was written in her mother's handwriting, and the message was both personal and urgent. The letter revealed that her mother had been trying to protect a crucial piece of information—a truth that, if uncovered, could put Ella's life in danger.

Ella and Tom continued to sift through the files, their sense of urgency growing with each new revelation. The hidden archive had provided them with valuable insights, but it also underscored the gravity of the situation. The mystery was far from over, and the threats they faced were becoming increasingly clear.

As they prepared to leave the warehouse, Ella felt a mix of apprehension and determination. The hidden archive had brought them closer to understanding the truth, but it also confirmed that they were up against a powerful and dangerous adversary. With new information in hand, they knew they had to stay one step ahead and uncover the full extent of the conspiracy that had entangled their lives.

7

Fractured Trust

Ella and Tom returned to their apartment with the newly discovered documents and the unsettling letter from Ella's mother. The night had fallen, shrouding the city in darkness. Ella's hands shook as she carefully placed the documents on the kitchen table. Each piece of paper was a fragment of a larger puzzle, and the letter from her mother only deepened the enigma they were facing.

Tom poured himself a cup of coffee, his gaze flicking nervously between the documents and Ella. "We need to make sense of all this. The letter was clear: your mother was trying to protect something important. But what?"

Ella nodded, her mind racing. "The letter mentioned a 'final key' that could expose everything. We need to figure out what that key is and how it fits into all this."

She began to sort through the documents, her flashlight casting a pale beam over the pages. The letter from her mother was particularly cryptic. It spoke of a "final key" that could unravel a conspiracy but didn't specify what the key was or where it could be found. The documents detailed various operations, codes, and meetings but lacked a clear, cohesive narrative.

As Ella reviewed the notes, she noticed a recurring name: Daniel Grey. His name appeared in several documents, often associated with high-level meetings and secret operations. Ella's stomach knotted. She had heard that name before—Daniel Grey was a well-known figure in the corporate world, often in the news for his philanthropic efforts. But the documents suggested he was involved in something far more sinister.

"Tom, I think we need to look into Daniel Grey," Ella said, her voice filled with determination. "The documents link him to all these operations. If anyone holds the 'final key,' it might be him."

Tom nodded, setting his coffee aside. "Alright, let's do some digging. But we need to be cautious. If he's involved, he might have connections and resources that we don't."

They spent the next few hours researching Daniel Grey. The more they uncovered, the more unsettling the picture became. Grey's public persona was immaculate—successful businessman, generous philanthropist, and respected leader. But the documents hinted at a darker side, suggesting that his public image was a carefully crafted facade hiding a more dangerous reality.

As dawn approached, Ella and Tom decided to visit Grey's corporate headquarters. The building was a sleek, modern structure in the heart of the city, a stark contrast to the decrepit warehouses they had recently explored. It was early, and the office was still quiet as they approached.

Tom drove up to the entrance, his nerves on edge. "Do you think he's in there? Should we just walk in and ask questions?"

Ella hesitated. "I don't think walking in will work. We need to be more strategic. Let's see if we can gather any information or find a way to get closer to him."

They decided to enter the building and blend in as best as they could. The lobby was elegant, with marble floors and high ceilings. They approached the receptionist, who greeted them with a polite but wary smile.

"Hi, we're here to inquire about Mr. Daniel Grey," Ella said, trying to sound professional. "We have some questions about his recent projects."

The receptionist's expression shifted from polite to guarded. "Mr. Grey is currently in a meeting. Do you have an appointment?"

Ella shook her head. "No, we don't, but it's quite urgent. We're working on a research project and need to speak with him as soon as possible."

The receptionist glanced at them uncertainly but didn't immediately dismiss them. "I'll see if I can schedule a brief meeting. Please wait here."

Ella and Tom took a seat in the lobby, their nerves fraying as they waited. The minutes ticked by slowly, each second filled with mounting tension. Finally, the receptionist returned, her face serious.

"I've managed to arrange a brief meeting with Mr. Grey. Please follow me."

Ella and Tom followed the receptionist to a private office on the top floor. The office was spacious and impeccably decorated, reflecting Grey's affluent status. They were ushered inside, where Daniel Grey awaited them behind a large, polished desk. He was impeccably dressed in a tailored suit, his demeanor calm and collected.

"Mr. Grey, thank you for meeting with us," Ella began, trying to keep her voice steady. "We're conducting research and have some questions about your recent projects and associations."

Grey's gaze was sharp, his eyes calculating. "I see. And what exactly are you researching?"

Ella hesitated, choosing her words carefully. "We've come across some documents that mention your involvement in various operations. We're trying to understand the connections and the nature of these operations."

Grey's expression remained neutral, but Ella noticed a flicker of recognition in his eyes. "I'm afraid I can't help you with that. My work is confidential and involves sensitive information."

Tom glanced at Ella, his anxiety palpable. "We understand the need for confidentiality, but these documents are linked to something much larger. We believe there might be important information that needs to be disclosed."

Grey's gaze hardened. "You're treading on dangerous ground. I suggest you be careful about what you're digging into. There are consequences for prying into matters that don't concern you."

Ella felt a chill run down her spine. Grey's warning was clear, and it only confirmed that they were getting closer to something significant—and perilous. "We're just trying to get answers. If there's nothing to hide, then we have nothing to worry about."

Grey's expression remained unreadable. "I have to attend to other matters now. If you need anything else, please contact my assistant."

Ella and Tom left the office, their minds racing. The encounter with Grey had been unsettling. His warning and evasive attitude suggested that he had a lot to hide. As they left the building, Ella's thoughts were filled with the implications of their meeting.

"Do you think he knows something about the final key?" Tom asked, his voice low.

Ella nodded. "I'm sure of it. But he's not going to make it easy for us. We need to find another way to uncover the truth."

As they left the corporate headquarters, Ella and Tom realized that their quest for answers had just become more dangerous. The fractured trust and the ominous warning from Daniel Grey were signs that they were delving into a web of deception and danger. They had to proceed with caution and find a way to expose the truth without falling into the traps set by those who wanted to keep it hidden.

8

The Unseen Hand

The tension was palpable in the small, dimly lit apartment as Ella and Tom reviewed their notes from the day's events. They had barely managed to evade a potential surveillance by the mysterious figure they had spotted earlier. The apartment, their temporary refuge, felt increasingly like a cage, the walls closing in as their investigation grew riskier.

Ella rubbed her temples, her exhaustion evident. "We're running in circles. We need something concrete, something that will give us a clear path forward."

Tom leaned against the table, flipping through the stack of documents they had recovered. "We know Kane's connected to the bigger picture, and we've seen he's well-protected. What if we're looking at this the wrong way? Maybe we should focus on his connections, not just him."

Ella nodded thoughtfully. "Yes, if Kane is as influential as the documents suggest, his associates or clients might have the missing pieces. Let's dig into his network."

They began researching Kane's known associates and business partners. The more they uncovered, the clearer it became that Kane was a linchpin in a complex web of influence and secrecy. One name kept coming up in relation to his work: Evelyn Marks, a high-profile attorney known for her involvement in legal battles concerning corporate secrecy and high-stakes negotiations.

"If anyone can help us navigate Kane's web, it's Evelyn Marks," Ella said. "She's probably one of the few people who could shed light on his operations."

Tom agreed. "Her office is in the city, isn't it? We should pay her a visit."

The next morning, Ella and Tom drove to Evelyn Marks' office. The building was an imposing structure of glass and steel, reflecting the power and prestige of its occupants. The lobby was immaculate, with polished floors and an air of restrained opulence. The receptionist greeted them with a practiced smile.

"Good morning," Ella said. "We'd like to speak with Ms. Marks. We're conducting research on some corporate matters and believe she might be able to help us."

The receptionist's smile faltered slightly. "Ms. Marks is in meetings all day. Do you have an appointment?"

Ella shook her head. "No, but it's quite urgent. We've come across some important information that might be relevant to her."

The receptionist's expression hardened, but she reluctantly took their contact information and promised to pass it along. Ella and Tom took a seat in the lobby, their anxiety growing as they waited. The minutes dragged by, the silence of the lobby feeling increasingly oppressive.

After a while, the receptionist returned, her demeanor more serious. "Ms. Marks has agreed to a brief meeting. Please follow me."

Ella and Tom followed the receptionist to an elevator that took them to a private floor. Evelyn Marks' office was as impressive as the rest of the building—large, well-furnished, with floor-to-ceiling windows offering a panoramic view of the city.

Ms. Marks, a woman in her late forties with an air of commanding authority, welcomed them with a courteous but distant demeanor. "Mr. Tom, Ms. Ella. Please, have a seat."

Ella and Tom took their seats across from Marks, trying to keep their composure. Ella introduced herself and Tom, explaining their interest in the connections between Kane and various operations.

Marks listened intently, her gaze sharp. "I see. And what exactly are you hoping to find out?"

"We've come across some documents suggesting that Kane is involved in several covert operations. We believe that understanding his connections might lead us to more information about a larger conspiracy," Ella explained.

Marks' expression remained inscrutable. "I'm familiar with Kane's reputation. He's involved in many high-profile cases, and his clients often require strict confidentiality. However, I can't divulge any details about his work or his associates."

Ella sensed that Marks was holding back. "We understand the need for confidentiality, but we're dealing with something that could be dangerous. Any information you could provide might help us prevent further issues."

Marks studied them carefully. "Dangerous, you say? It sounds like you're delving into matters that are beyond your control. Are you aware of the risks involved?"

Ella nodded. "We are. But we're committed to uncovering the truth."

Marks leaned back in her chair, her fingers steepled as she considered their request. "I can't directly assist you with Kane's affairs. However, there might be another way to approach this."

She reached into her desk drawer and pulled out a small, sealed envelope. "Inside this envelope is information that might be useful. It's not directly related to Kane but pertains to the broader network he's part of. Use it wisely."

Ella took the envelope, her curiosity piqued. "Thank you. We'll be careful with it."

As they left Marks' office, Ella and Tom examined the envelope. It was unmarked, its contents unknown. They decided to open it once they were back at their apartment.

On the way back, Tom drove in silence, his mind occupied with the potential implications of the envelope. "Do you think this information could be a game-changer?"

Ella's face was tense. "It might be. We need to review it carefully and see if it offers any new leads or insights."

Back at the apartment, they carefully opened the envelope. Inside, they found a series of documents and a brief note. The documents contained detailed records of financial transactions, contracts, and meeting minutes related to various operations. One name repeatedly appeared in the records—Rebecca Cross, a journalist known for investigating corporate corruption and hidden agendas.

The note was brief but ominous: "Rebecca Cross might be able to provide further insights. She has connections and information that could be crucial."

Ella's eyes widened. "Rebecca Cross? She's well-known for uncovering corporate scandals. If she's involved, she might have valuable information about the network we're investigating."

Tom nodded. "It looks like we need to reach out to her. She might be able to connect the dots and provide the clarity we need."

As they prepared to contact Rebecca Cross, Ella and Tom knew they were entering a new phase of their investigation. The information from Evelyn Marks was a significant lead, but it also brought new challenges. They were venturing deeper into a world of shadows and deceit, and their quest for the truth was becoming increasingly perilous.

The unseen hand guiding their investigation was becoming more apparent, and with every step, the stakes were rising. Ella and Tom had to stay vigilant and navigate the treacherous waters of corporate secrecy and corruption. The path ahead was fraught with danger, but the pursuit of truth drove them forward, no matter the risks they faced.

9

The Unseen Hand

The tension was palpable in the small, dimly lit apartment as Ella and Tom reviewed their notes from the day's events. They had barely managed to evade a potential surveillance by the mysterious figure they had spotted earlier. The apartment, their temporary refuge, felt increasingly like a cage, the walls closing in as their investigation grew riskier.

Ella rubbed her temples, her exhaustion evident. "We're running in circles. We need something concrete, something that will give us a clear path forward."

Tom leaned against the table, flipping through the stack of documents they had recovered. "We know Kane's connected to the bigger picture, and we've seen he's well-protected. What if we're looking at this the wrong way? Maybe we should focus on his connections, not just him."

Ella nodded thoughtfully. "Yes, if Kane is as influential as the documents suggest, his associates or clients might have the missing pieces. Let's dig into his network."

They began researching Kane's known associates and business partners. The more they uncovered, the clearer it became that Kane was a linchpin in a complex web of influence and secrecy. One name kept coming up in relation to his work: Evelyn Marks, a high-profile attorney known for her involvement in legal battles concerning corporate secrecy and high-stakes negotiations.

"If anyone can help us navigate Kane's web, it's Evelyn Marks," Ella said. "She's probably one of the few people who could shed light on his operations."

Tom agreed. "Her office is in the city, isn't it? We should pay her a visit."

The next morning, Ella and Tom drove to Evelyn Marks' office. The building was an imposing structure of glass and steel, reflecting the power and prestige of its occupants. The lobby was immaculate, with polished floors and an air of restrained opulence. The receptionist greeted them with a practiced smile.

"Good morning," Ella said. "We'd like to speak with Ms. Marks. We're conducting research on some corporate matters and believe she might be able to help us."

The receptionist's smile faltered slightly. "Ms. Marks is in meetings all day. Do you have an appointment?"

Ella shook her head. "No, but it's quite urgent. We've come across some important information that might be relevant to her."

The receptionist's expression hardened, but she reluctantly took their contact information and promised to pass it along. Ella and Tom took a seat in the lobby, their anxiety growing as they waited. The minutes dragged by, the silence of the lobby feeling increasingly oppressive.

After a while, the receptionist returned, her demeanor more serious. "Ms. Marks has agreed to a brief meeting. Please follow me."

Ella and Tom followed the receptionist to an elevator that took them to a private floor. Evelyn Marks' office was as impressive as the rest of the building—large, well-furnished, with floor-to-ceiling windows offering a panoramic view of the city.

Ms. Marks, a woman in her late forties with an air of commanding authority, welcomed them with a courteous but distant demeanor. "Mr. Tom, Ms. Ella. Please, have a seat."

Ella and Tom took their seats across from Marks, trying to keep their composure. Ella introduced herself and Tom, explaining their interest in the connections between Kane and various operations.

Marks listened intently, her gaze sharp. "I see. And what exactly are you hoping to find out?"

"We've come across some documents suggesting that Kane is involved in several covert operations. We believe that understanding his connections might lead us to more information about a larger conspiracy," Ella explained.

Marks' expression remained inscrutable. "I'm familiar with Kane's reputation. He's involved in many high-profile cases, and his clients often require strict confidentiality. However, I can't divulge any details about his work or his associates."

Ella sensed that Marks was holding back. "We understand the need for confidentiality, but we're dealing with something that could be dangerous. Any information you could provide might help us prevent further issues."

Marks studied them carefully. "Dangerous, you say? It sounds like you're delving into matters that are beyond your control. Are you aware of the risks involved?"

Ella nodded. "We are. But we're committed to uncovering the truth."

Marks leaned back in her chair, her fingers steepled as she considered their request. "I can't directly assist you with Kane's affairs. However, there might be another way to approach this."

She reached into her desk drawer and pulled out a small, sealed envelope. "Inside this envelope is information that might be useful. It's not directly related to Kane but pertains to the broader network he's part of. Use it wisely."

Ella took the envelope, her curiosity piqued. "Thank you. We'll be careful with it."

As they left Marks' office, Ella and Tom examined the envelope. It was unmarked, its contents unknown. They decided to open it once they were back at their apartment.

On the way back, Tom drove in silence, his mind occupied with the potential implications of the envelope. "Do you think this information could be a game-changer?"

Ella's face was tense. "It might be. We need to review it carefully and see if it offers any new leads or insights."

Back at the apartment, they carefully opened the envelope. Inside, they found a series of documents and a brief note. The documents contained detailed records of financial transactions, contracts, and meeting minutes related to various operations. One name repeatedly appeared in the records—Rebecca Cross, a journalist known for investigating corporate corruption and hidden agendas.

The note was brief but ominous: "Rebecca Cross might be able to provide further insights. She has connections and information that could be crucial."

Ella's eyes widened. "Rebecca Cross? She's well-known for uncovering corporate scandals. If she's involved, she might have valuable information about the network we're investigating."

Tom nodded. "It looks like we need to reach out to her. She might be able to connect the dots and provide the clarity we need."

As they prepared to contact Rebecca Cross, Ella and Tom knew they were entering a new phase of their investigation. The information from Evelyn Marks was a significant lead, but it also brought new challenges. They were venturing deeper into a world of shadows and deceit, and their quest for the truth was becoming increasingly perilous.

The unseen hand guiding their investigation was becoming more apparent, and with every step, the stakes were rising. Ella and Tom had to stay vigilant and navigate the treacherous waters of corporate secrecy and corruption. The path ahead was fraught with danger, but the pursuit of truth drove them forward, no matter the risks they faced.

10

Echoes of the Past

The apartment was cloaked in the hush of early morning as Ella and Tom reviewed the information they had gathered. The documents from Evelyn Marks had introduced a new dimension to their investigation, but the real breakthrough seemed to lie with Rebecca Cross. The journalist's reputation for exposing corporate corruption made her a critical lead, and Ella's instincts told her that contacting Cross was essential.

Ella picked up her phone and dialed the number provided in the documents. It rang several times before being answered by a gruff voice.

"Rebecca Cross."

"Ms. Cross, my name is Ella Harcourt. I'm working on a research project related to corporate corruption and came across your name. I believe you might have information that could be crucial to our investigation."

There was a brief silence on the other end of the line. "What kind of information?"

Ella hesitated. "We've uncovered a network involving several high-profile figures. Your name was mentioned in connection with this network. We need to discuss it further."

"Meet me at the Central Café in one hour," Cross replied curtly before hanging up.

Ella and Tom made their way to the Central Café, a quaint establishment nestled between towering skyscrapers. Its unassuming appearance contrasted sharply with the high-stakes world they were delving into. The café was quiet, with only a few early patrons sipping their coffee.

Ella and Tom arrived early and chose a secluded table at the back. They waited in tense anticipation, their nerves frayed by the importance of this meeting. As the clock approached their appointed time, the café door opened, and Rebecca Cross walked in.

She was in her late thirties, with a sharp, analytical gaze and a demeanor that commanded respect. Dressed in a dark coat and carrying a weathered briefcase, she looked every bit the seasoned journalist. Ella and Tom stood to greet her.

"Ms. Cross, thank you for meeting with us," Ella said as she extended her hand.

Cross shook Ella's hand briefly before taking a seat. "Let's get down to business. What do you have?"

Ella and Tom shared their findings and explained their current situation, focusing on the connections between Kane, Marks, and the broader network. Cross listened intently, her eyes flicking to the documents they had brought along.

"I've been tracking similar leads for some time," Cross said. "The network you're dealing with is vast and well-protected. Kane is just one piece of a much larger puzzle. What exactly are you hoping to uncover?"

"We're trying to find out more about the 'final key' mentioned in the documents and how it relates to the conspiracy," Ella explained. "We believe it's tied to a significant cover-up or operation."

Cross's expression grew serious. "The final key. That's a term I've heard before. It's often used as a euphemism for something highly sensitive—something that, if exposed, could have major repercussions."

Ella's heart raced. "Do you know what it might be?"

Cross hesitated before answering. "I've come across references to a final key in various investigations. It often involves hidden agendas and covert operations. In one case, it was linked to illegal financial transactions and secret agreements between powerful figures."

Tom leaned in. "We've also encountered a name—Evelyn Marks. She seems to be deeply involved in this network."

Cross's eyes narrowed. "Marks is a significant player. Her role in maintaining secrecy for powerful clients cannot be underestimated. If she's involved, then the stakes are even higher."

Ella nodded. "We've met with her. She provided us with information about Robert Kane and suggested contacting you. She implied that you might have further insights into this network."

Cross leaned back in her chair, her gaze thoughtful. "I've been investigating this network for years. It's a complex web involving several high-profile individuals and organizations. The 'final key' could be a crucial piece of evidence that links these figures together."

Ella felt a surge of hope. "Do you have any leads or information that could help us?"

Cross considered the question carefully. "I have some contacts who might be able to provide additional information. But be warned—this is a dangerous path. The people involved in this network are ruthless and will go to great lengths to protect their secrets."

Ella and Tom exchanged a worried glance. "We're prepared for the risks," Ella said. "We need to find the truth, no matter what."

Cross nodded. "Alright. I'll reach out to my contacts and see what I can find out. In the meantime, be careful. The network you're dealing with is not to be underestimated."

As Cross prepared to leave, Ella noticed a shadowy figure watching them from across the café. The figure was partially obscured by a newspaper, but Ella could sense a malevolent presence. The figure's gaze seemed to follow their every move, heightening Ella's sense of unease.

"Ms. Cross, thank you for your help," Ella said, trying to keep her voice steady.

Cross gave a curt nod. "Be careful. And remember, not everything is as it seems."

After Cross left, Ella and Tom remained in the café, their minds racing. The encounter with Cross had provided valuable insights, but it also heightened their sense of danger. The shadowy figure observing them was a stark reminder of the risks they faced.

As they left the café, Ella and Tom were acutely aware of the potential threats surrounding them. The investigation was leading them deeper into a dangerous world of secrecy and corruption, and their every move was being watched.

Back at their apartment, they reviewed their notes and discussed their next steps. The information from Cross was crucial, but it was clear that they were entering a more perilous phase of their investigation. The final key was still elusive, but the pieces of the puzzle were beginning to fall into place.

Ella and Tom knew that they had to stay vigilant and continue their pursuit of the truth, despite the growing risks. The echoes of the past were becoming more pronounced, and the shadowy figures lurking in the background were a constant reminder of the dangers that lay ahead. The quest for truth was fraught with peril, but they were determined to uncover the hidden realities and bring the conspiracy to light.

11

The Veil Lifts

The city skyline was bathed in twilight as Ella and Tom sat in their apartment, the tension in the room almost tangible. The meeting with Rebecca Cross had shed some light on their investigation, but it also revealed the depth of the danger they were facing. The shadowy figure in the café lingered in their minds, a stark reminder of the threats that lay ahead.

Ella was pacing the room, the documents from Cross and Marks spread out on the table. She glanced at the clock—almost midnight. Tom, seated at the table, was absorbed in examining the papers.

"We need to figure out our next move," Ella said, her voice filled with determination. "Cross mentioned that she would reach out to her contacts. Maybe she'll come up with something concrete."

Tom looked up from the documents, his face etched with concern. "We can't rely solely on her. We need to be proactive. If we're getting closer to the truth, we should prepare for any potential threats."

Ella nodded. "I agree. Let's review everything we have. There might be something we missed, some connection we haven't explored."

They spent the next few hours meticulously combing through the documents. Ella was lost in thought when her phone buzzed, jolting her back to reality. It was a message from Rebecca Cross.

"Meet me at the old warehouse district. There's something you need to see. Be discreet."

Ella's heart raced. The warehouse district was a neglected area of the city, known for its abandoned buildings and derelict warehouses. It was a place where shady deals and illicit activities were rumored to take place.

"Tom, we need to go," Ella said, showing him the message. "Cross has found something. It could be crucial."

Tom grabbed his jacket and followed Ella as they made their way to the car. The drive to the warehouse district was filled with an uneasy silence, the streets growing darker and more desolate as they approached their destination.

When they arrived, the area was eerily quiet, the only sounds being the distant hum of traffic and the occasional rustle of wind through the broken windows of the abandoned buildings. They parked a few blocks away and walked cautiously toward the address Cross had provided.

The warehouse loomed ahead, a massive structure with crumbling walls and boarded-up windows. Ella and Tom approached the entrance, their steps echoing in the emptiness. They carefully pried open a side door and slipped inside.

The interior was dimly lit, the only light coming from a flickering bulb hanging from the ceiling. The air was thick with dust and the smell of decay. They moved silently through the maze of old crates and machinery, their senses heightened.

Suddenly, a figure emerged from the shadows—Rebecca Cross. Her expression was tense, her eyes scanning the area as if expecting trouble.

"Over here," Cross whispered, leading them to a secluded corner of the warehouse.

In the corner, there was a table covered with documents and photographs. Cross gestured for them to examine the materials.

"I managed to get hold of some sensitive files," Cross said, her voice low. "These are records of meetings and transactions related to the network you've been investigating."

Ella and Tom began to sift through the documents. They were detailed and extensive, showing a complex web of connections between various figures, including Robert Kane and Evelyn Marks. There were also references to secret meetings and covert operations.

One document caught Ella's eye—a list of names and code words linked to different operations. Among the names was a contact labeled "The Architect." The code words and references suggested that "The Architect" was a key figure in orchestrating the network's operations.

"This could be the breakthrough we need," Tom said, pointing to the document. "If we can identify 'The Architect,' we might be able to unravel the whole conspiracy."

As they continued to examine the materials, a sudden noise behind them made them freeze. The sound of footsteps echoed through the warehouse, growing louder and closer. Ella's heart pounded as she glanced at Cross.

"Someone's coming," Cross said urgently. "We need to get out of here."

Ella and Tom quickly gathered the documents and followed Cross through the maze of crates and machinery. The footsteps were growing nearer, and the sense of danger was palpable.

They reached a back exit and slipped through it, emerging into a narrow alleyway. The alley was dark, and the shadows seemed to close in around them. They moved quickly, their breaths visible in the cold air.

"We need to find a safe place to go through these documents," Ella said as they reached the end of the alley. "Somewhere we can stay hidden and analyze the information."

Tom nodded, glancing around the darkened street. "Let's head to the office. It's secure and private."

They made their way to their office, their nerves on edge. Once inside, they spread out the documents and photographs on their desk. The evidence was compelling, but they needed to process it carefully to avoid missing any critical details.

Ella focused on the document mentioning "The Architect." The name was shrouded in secrecy, but the connections and code words hinted at a powerful and influential figure behind the scenes.

As they worked late into the night, a feeling of urgency gripped them. The pieces of the puzzle were starting to come together, but the risk of exposure was growing. They were getting closer to uncovering the truth, but the dangers of their pursuit were becoming more apparent.

The veil was lifting, revealing the hidden world of deceit and corruption they were uncovering. Ella and Tom knew that they were on the brink of a significant revelation, but they also understood that the final steps of their investigation would be the most perilous. The search for "The Architect" would likely lead them into deeper danger, and they had to remain vigilant to navigate the treacherous path ahead.

12

The Architect's Labyrinth

Ella and Tom were up before dawn, their nerves frayed from the night's events. The documents Rebecca Cross had provided were spread across their office floor, illuminated by the weak light of a desk lamp. Each page seemed to whisper secrets, promising to unveil the elusive figure known as "The Architect."

Tom's hands shook slightly as he flipped through the papers. "This is a goldmine of information. If we can decipher these code words and connections, we might finally understand the full extent of the network."

Ella nodded, her eyes scanning a map included in the documents. It depicted various locations marked with cryptic symbols and lines connecting them. At the center of the map was a location labeled "Nexus," surrounded by several other points of interest.

"The Nexus," Ella murmured. "It looks like it's the central hub of this entire operation. If we can figure out what's significant about this place, we might be able to locate The Architect."

Tom leaned in closer, examining a series of photographs attached to the documents. "These photos show meetings at various locations. Some of them are taken from angles that suggest surveillance. It's like someone was keeping tabs on the participants."

Ella's eyes narrowed. "If The Architect is behind this, they must have a secure way of managing their operations. These locations and meetings could provide us with a direct link to them."

As they continued their analysis, a sudden knock at the office door made them freeze. Tom glanced at Ella, their earlier caution returning. They had been careful to avoid detection, but the knock was a jarring reminder that they were not alone in their pursuit.

Ella approached the door cautiously and peered through the peephole. The hallway outside was empty, but the sense of unease lingered. "It could be someone trying to find us or someone who knows what we're up to."

Tom moved to a window, checking the street below. "I don't see anything unusual. Maybe it's just a delivery or someone who's mistaken our office for another."

They decided to take a precautionary approach. Ella turned off the lights and they hid behind a stack of file cabinets, waiting in silence. The seconds felt like hours as they listened intently for any signs of intrusion.

After several tense minutes, the knocking stopped. Ella slowly approached the door and opened it slightly, peering into the hallway. To their relief, there was no one in sight. However, the feeling of being watched persisted.

"Let's not take any chances," Ella said. "We need to find out what's really going on. We should use the map and investigate the Nexus location."

Tom nodded, and they quickly gathered their materials and left the office, taking care to ensure they weren't followed. The Nexus on the map was located in an industrial area on the outskirts of the city. It was known for its large warehouses and low foot traffic—a perfect location for covert activities.

As they approached the area, the sky was overcast, casting a gray pallor over the deserted streets. The industrial buildings loomed like silent sentinels, their windows dark and foreboding. Ella and Tom parked a few blocks away and made their way toward the designated location.

The Nexus was situated in an old, repurposed warehouse with no distinguishing features. The entrance was heavily fortified with security cameras and motion sensors. It was clear that the place was well-protected.

"We need to be careful," Ella said. "If this is indeed the central hub, it could be crawling with security."

Tom scanned the perimeter, noting several surveillance cameras mounted around the building. "We should look for a way in that avoids detection. There must be a back entrance or a weak spot in the security."

They circled the warehouse, searching for any potential entry points. Their patience paid off when they discovered a small, partially hidden door at the rear of the building. It appeared to be used for deliveries, and the security measures here were less stringent.

Ella and Tom waited until the area was clear and then approached the door. Tom used a lock-picking set to open it, and they slipped inside, their hearts racing with adrenaline.

The interior of the warehouse was cavernous and dimly lit. Stacks of crates and machinery created a maze-like environment. The air was thick with dust, and the only sounds were the occasional creaks of the building settling.

They moved cautiously through the warehouse, guided by the map and the information from the documents. The Nexus was marked on the map as a central control room, so they headed in that direction, their movements as silent as possible.

As they neared their destination, they noticed a series of locked doors and security panels. They used a combination of stealth and quick thinking to bypass the security measures. Each success brought them closer to their goal, but the risk of being discovered remained high.

Finally, they reached a large, reinforced door marked with the emblem of a key. Tom used a combination of codes and lock-picking techniques to gain access. The door creaked open, revealing a high-tech control room filled with monitors, computers, and files.

"This must be it," Ella said, her voice barely above a whisper. "This is where The Architect manages everything."

They began to sift through the files and data on the computers. The screens displayed surveillance footage, detailed records of meetings, and coded messages. Ella's eyes widened as she spotted a familiar name on one of the screens: "Rebecca Cross."

"Cross is being monitored," Tom said, his voice tense. "It looks like they've been keeping tabs on everyone involved."

Ella accessed a file labeled "The Architect." It contained detailed plans, names, and operations related to the conspiracy. The Architect's identity was still hidden behind layers of code and encryption, but there were clues suggesting a high-ranking corporate figure with significant influence.

Before they could delve deeper, a sudden noise from outside the control room made them freeze. The sound of footsteps and voices approached rapidly.

"We've been compromised," Ella said, panic in her voice. "We need to get out of here now!"

Tom quickly shut down the computers and gathered the documents. They retraced their steps through the maze of crates and machinery, their hearts pounding with urgency. The footsteps grew louder, and the risk of capture was imminent.

They reached the rear door and slipped outside, their escape just in time. As they fled the warehouse, Ella and Tom felt a surge of both relief and dread. They had uncovered significant information, but their narrow escape was a stark reminder of the dangers they faced.

Back in their car, they reviewed the documents and data they had managed to secure. The Nexus had provided a crucial lead, but the identity of The Architect remained elusive. The pursuit of the truth was growing more perilous, and the web of deceit was becoming more entangled.

Ella and Tom knew they had to continue their investigation with renewed determination. The Architect's labyrinth was a formidable challenge, but they were committed to unraveling the conspiracy, no matter the risks. The secrets they had uncovered were just the beginning, and the path ahead would test their resolve like never before.